GRAPHIC SCIENCE

THE DYNAMIC WORLD OF

CHEMICAL REACTIONS

WITH MAX AXIOM SUPER SCIENTIST

by Agnieszka Biskup

illustrated by Cynthia Martin and Barbara Schulz

Consultant:
Leslie Flynn, PhD
Science Education, Chemistry
University of Minnesota
Twin Cities Campus

CAPSTONE PRESS
a capstone imprint

Graphic Library is published by Capstone Press,
151 Good Counsel Drive, P.O. Box 669, Mankato, Minnesota 56002.
www.capstonepub.com

Books published by Capstone Press are manufactured with paper
containing at least 10 percent post-consumer waste.

Library of Congress Cataloging-in-Publication Data
Biskup, Agnieszka.
  The dynamic world of chemical reactions with Max Axiom, super scientist / by Agnieszka
Biskup ; illustrated by Cynthia Martin and Barbara Schulz.
    p. cm.—(Graphic library. Graphic science)
  Summary: "In graphic novel format, follows the adventures of Max Axiom as he explores
the science of chemical reactions"—Provided by publisher.
  Includes bibliographical references and index.
  ISBN 978-1-4296-4772-4 (library binding)
  ISBN 978-1-4296-5635-1 (paperback)
  1. Chemical reactions—Comic books, strips, etc.—Juvenile literature. I. Martin, Cynthia,
1961– ill. II. Schulz, Barbara (Barbara Jo), ill. III. Title. IV. Series.
  QD501.B677 2011
  541'.39—dc22   2010000557

Designer
Alison Thiele

Media Researcher
Wanda Winch

Cover Artists
Tod G. Smith and Krista Ward

Production Specialist
Laura Manthe

Colorist
Matt Webb

Editor
Christopher L. Harbo

Photo illustration credits: Shutterstock/Natalia Klenova, 6; Orca, 12, 13

Printed in the United States of America in Stevens Point, Wisconsin.
012011
006049R

TABLE OF CONTENTS

SECTION 1

REACTIONS AROUND US---------- 4

SECTION 2

MATTER, ATOMS, AND MOLECULES--- 8

SECTION 3

CHANGING MATTER ---------------14

SECTION 4

DYNAMIC REACTIONS------------ 22

More about Chemical Reactions and Max Axiom 28–29
Glossary 30
Read More 31
Internet Sites 31
Index 32

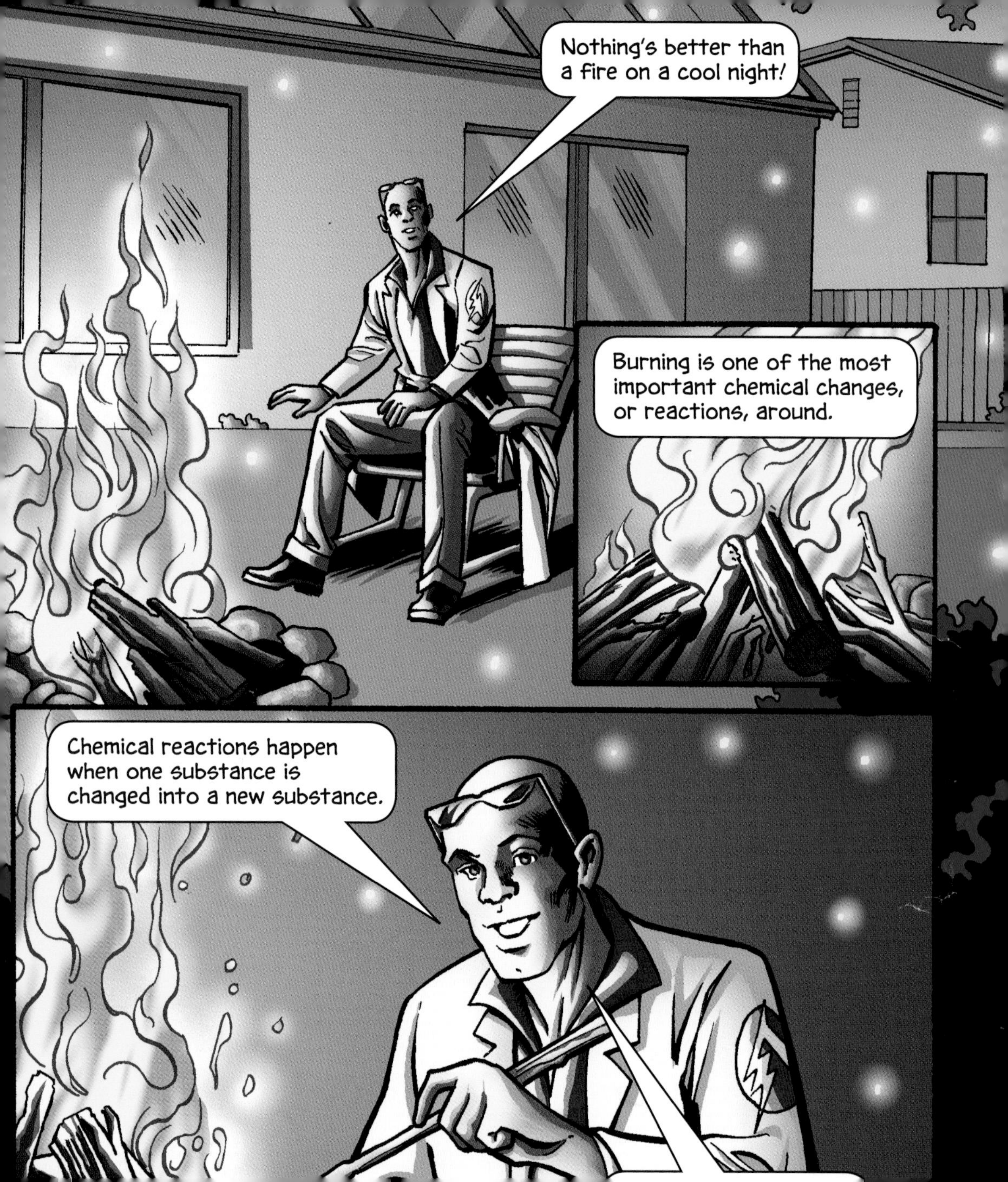
Nothing's better than a fire on a cool night!
Burning is one of the most important chemical changes, or reactions, around.
Chemical reactions happen when one substance is changed into a new substance.

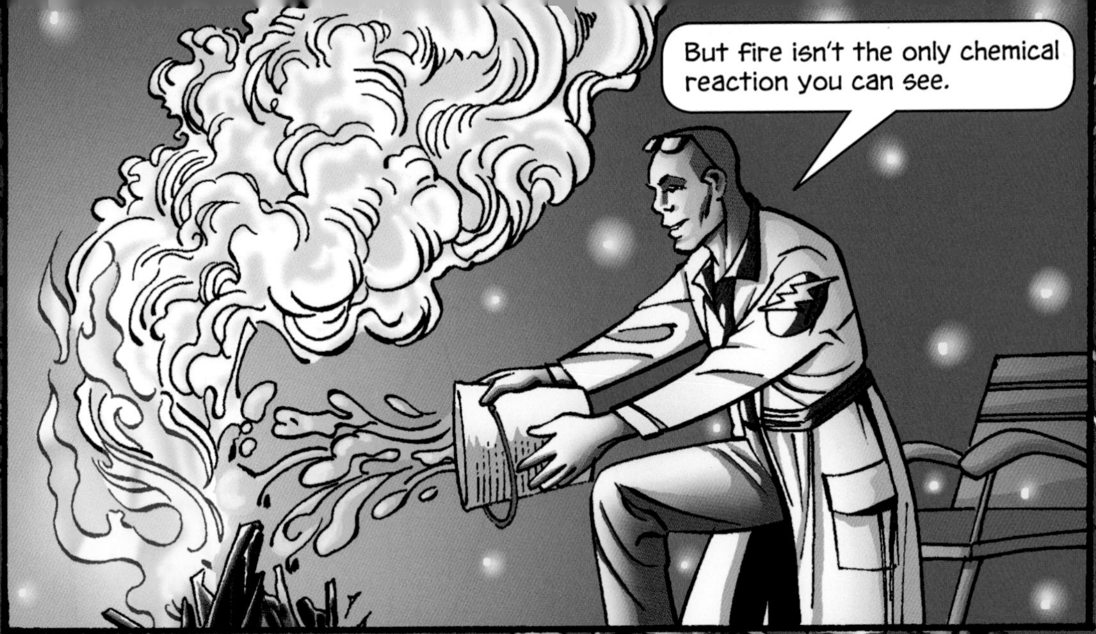
But fire isn't the only chemical reaction you can see.

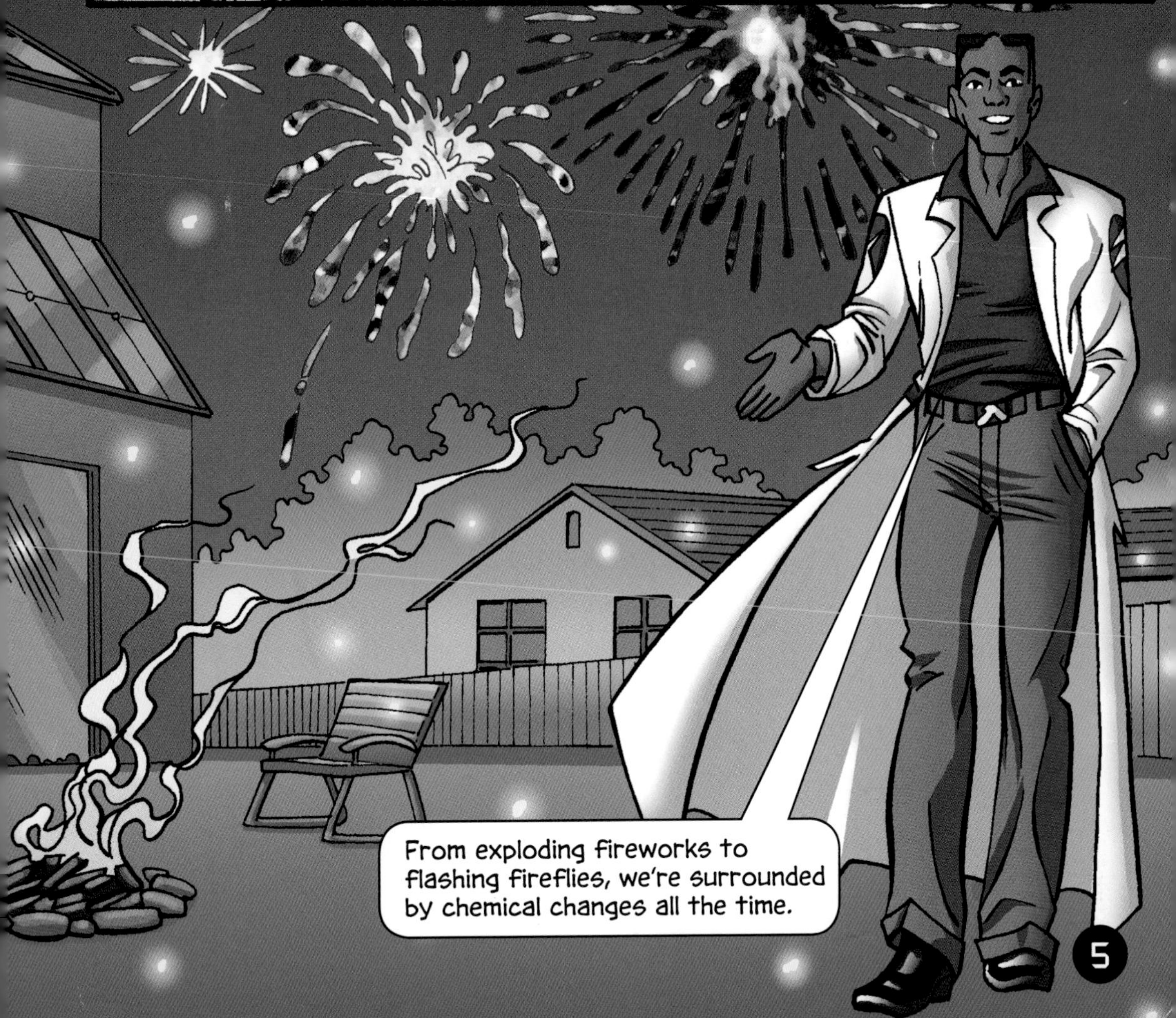
From exploding fireworks to flashing fireflies, we're surrounded by chemical changes all the time.

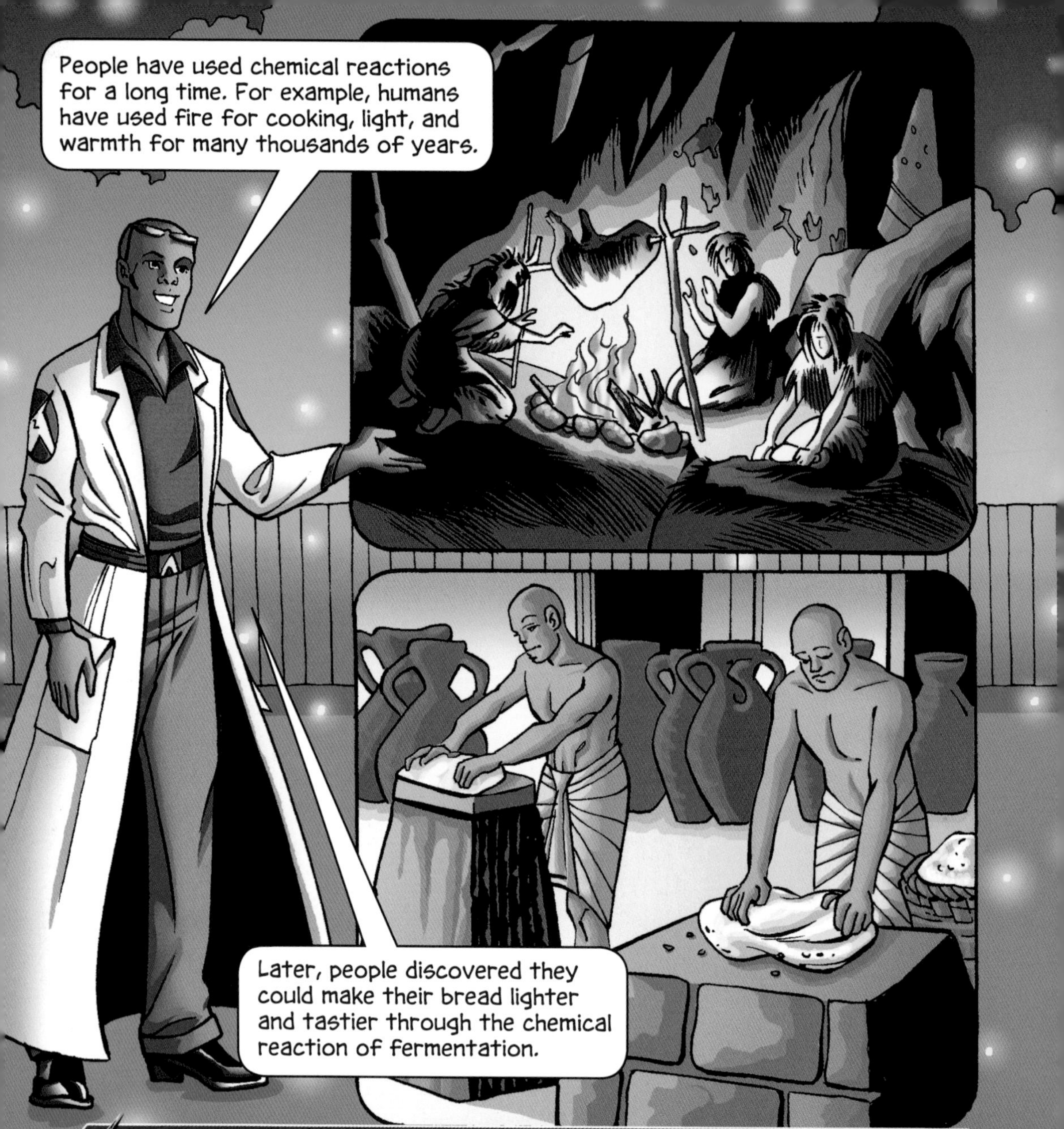
People have used chemical reactions for a long time. For example, humans have used fire for cooking, light, and warmth for many thousands of years.
Later, people discovered they could make their bread lighter and tastier through the chemical reaction of fermentation.

FERMENTATION

ACCESS GRANTED: MAX AXIOM

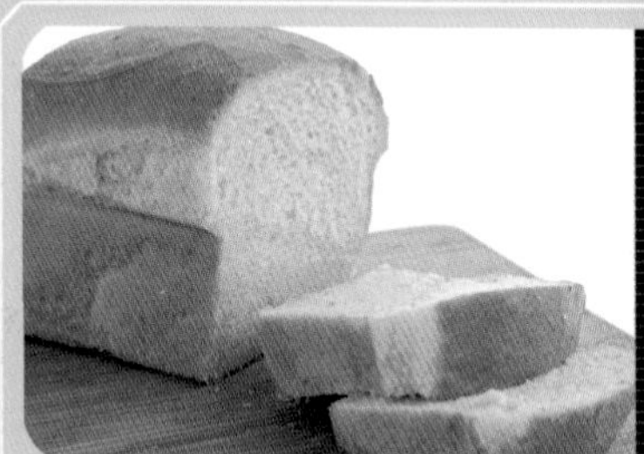

Fermentation can be used to produce various foods and beverages. It results when bacteria or yeast digest simple sugars. This digestion process gives off carbon dioxide gas and ethyl alcohol. It is the release of carbon dioxide gas that makes bread dough rise.

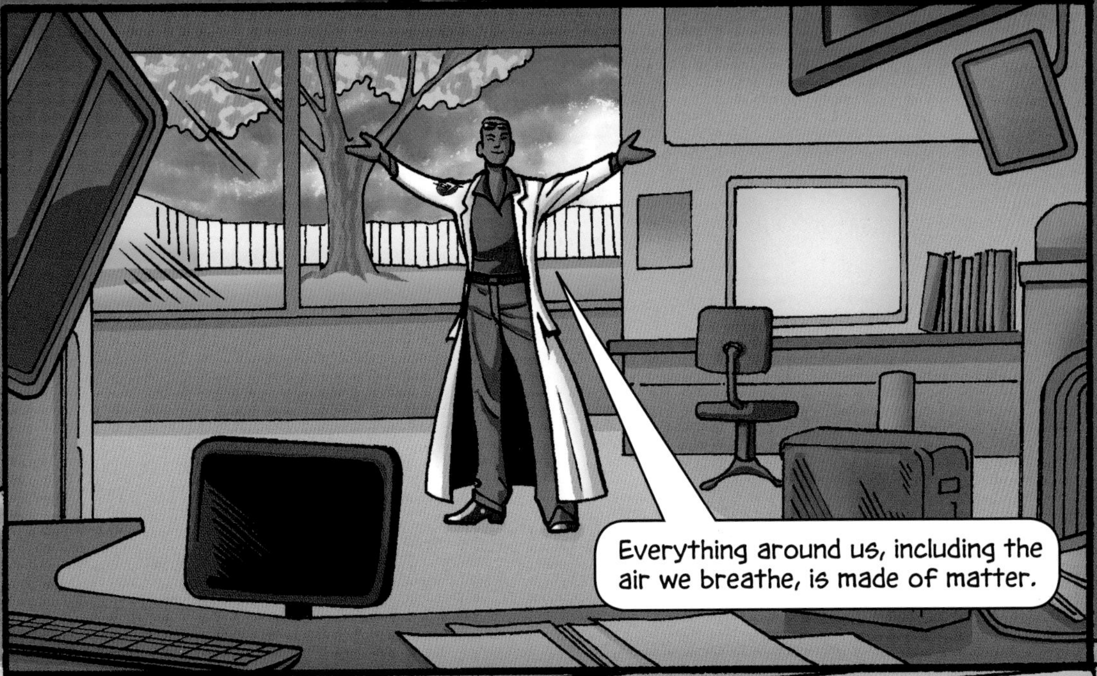
Everything around us, including the air we breathe, is made of matter.

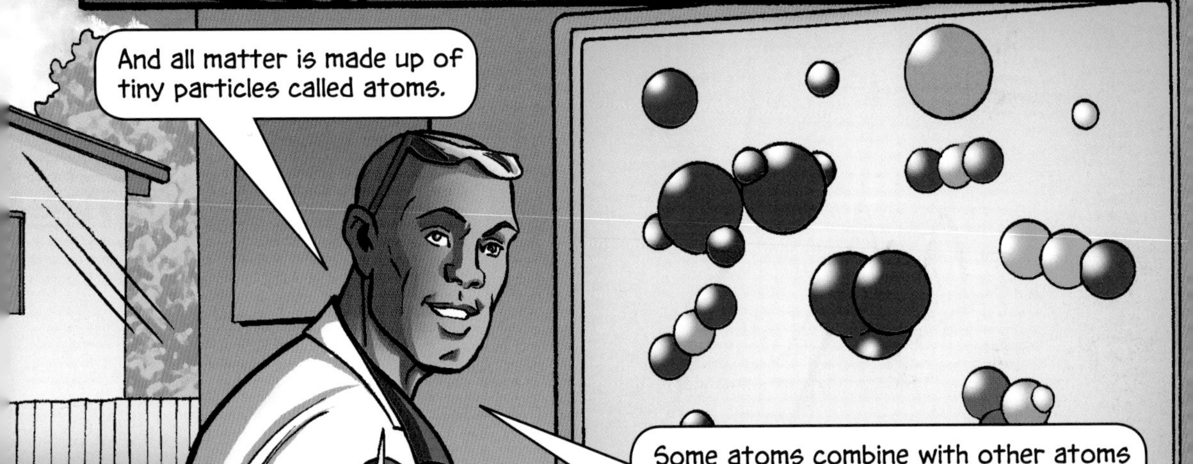
And all matter is made up of tiny particles called atoms.
Some atoms combine with other atoms and stick together in groups called molecules. Let's see how they work.

INSIDE THE ATOM

ACCESS GRANTED: MAX AXIOM

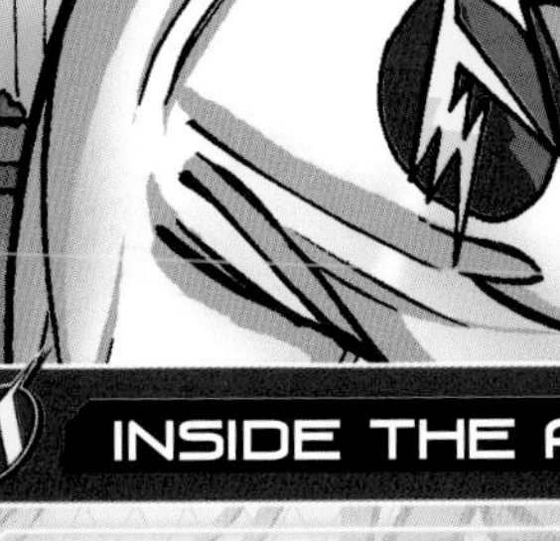

Atoms can be broken down into even smaller particles called neutrons, protons, and electrons. Protons and neutrons stick together at the center of the atom, called the nucleus. Electrons whiz superfast all around the nucleus.

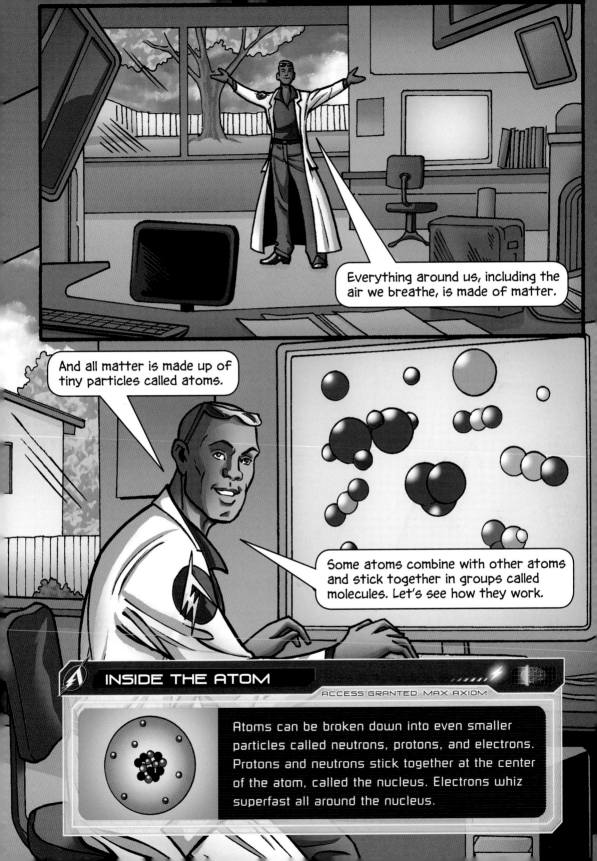

Imagine taking a drop of water and splitting it in two.

Now split it again ...

... and again and again.

Eventually you'd split the drop down to a single molecule of water.

H

H

O

And if you looked closely, you'd see its basic structure. A water molecule is made up of one oxygen atom and two hydrogen atoms.

TINY, TINY ATOMS

It can be mind-boggling to think about the very small size of atoms. There can be a few sextillion (a 1 followed by 21 zeros) atoms in a drop of water. Can you imagine 1,000,000,000,000,000,000,000 of anything?

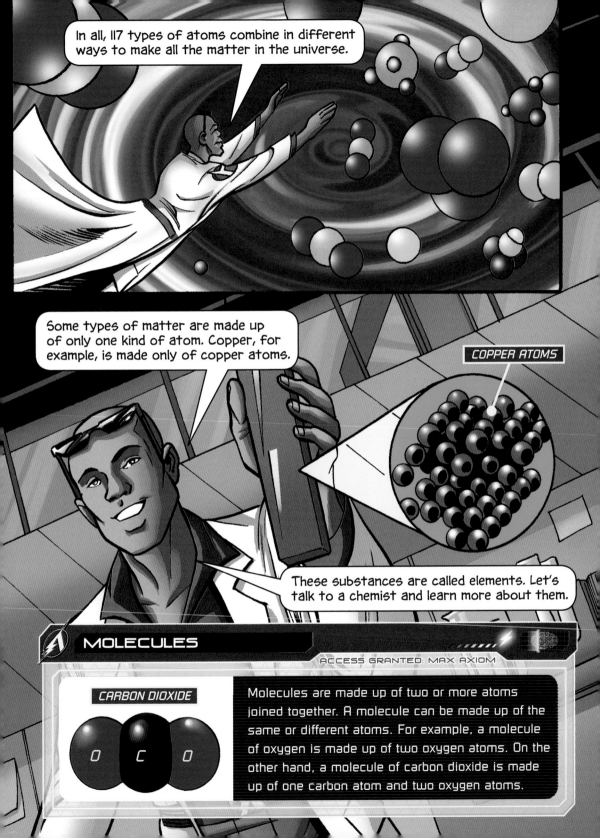

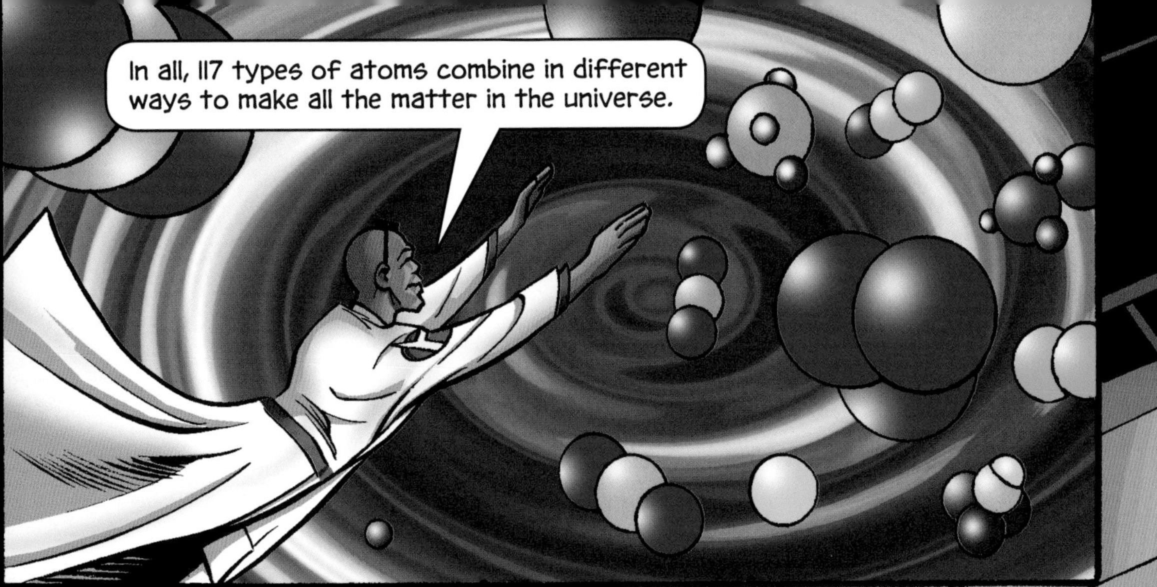
In all, 117 types of atoms combine in different ways to make all the matter in the universe.

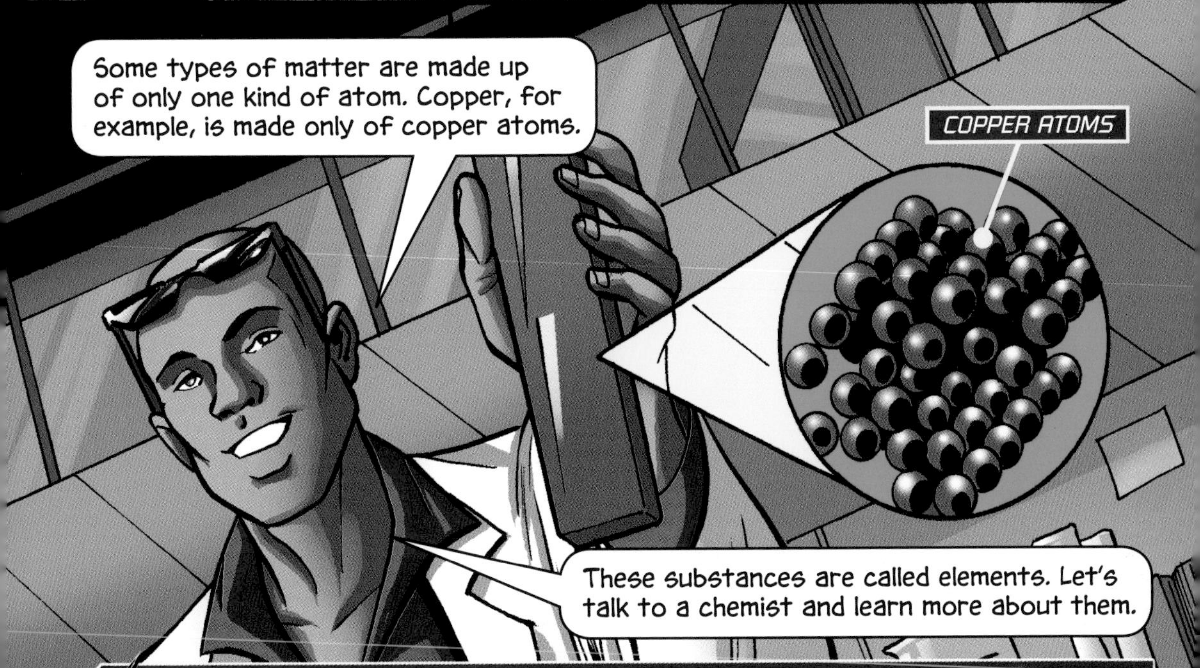
Some types of matter are made up of only one kind of atom. Copper, for example, is made only of copper atoms.
COPPER ATOMS
These substances are called elements. Let's talk to a chemist and learn more about them.

MOLECULES

ACCESS GRANTED: MAX AXIOM

CARBON DIOXIDE

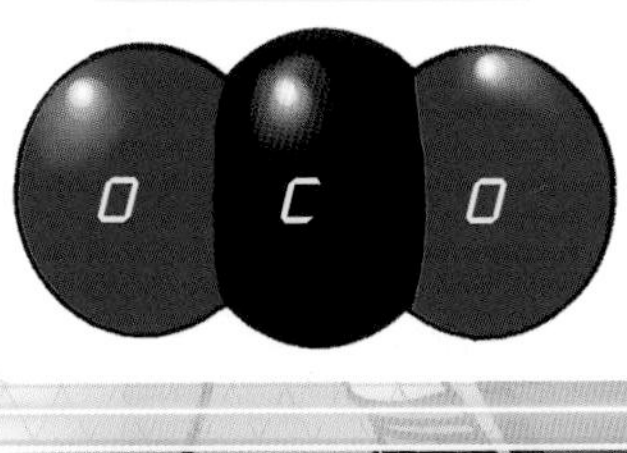
O
C
O

Molecules are made up of two or more atoms joined together. A molecule can be made up of the same or different atoms. For example, a molecule of oxygen is made up of two oxygen atoms. On the other hand, a molecule of carbon dioxide is made up of one carbon atom and two oxygen atoms.

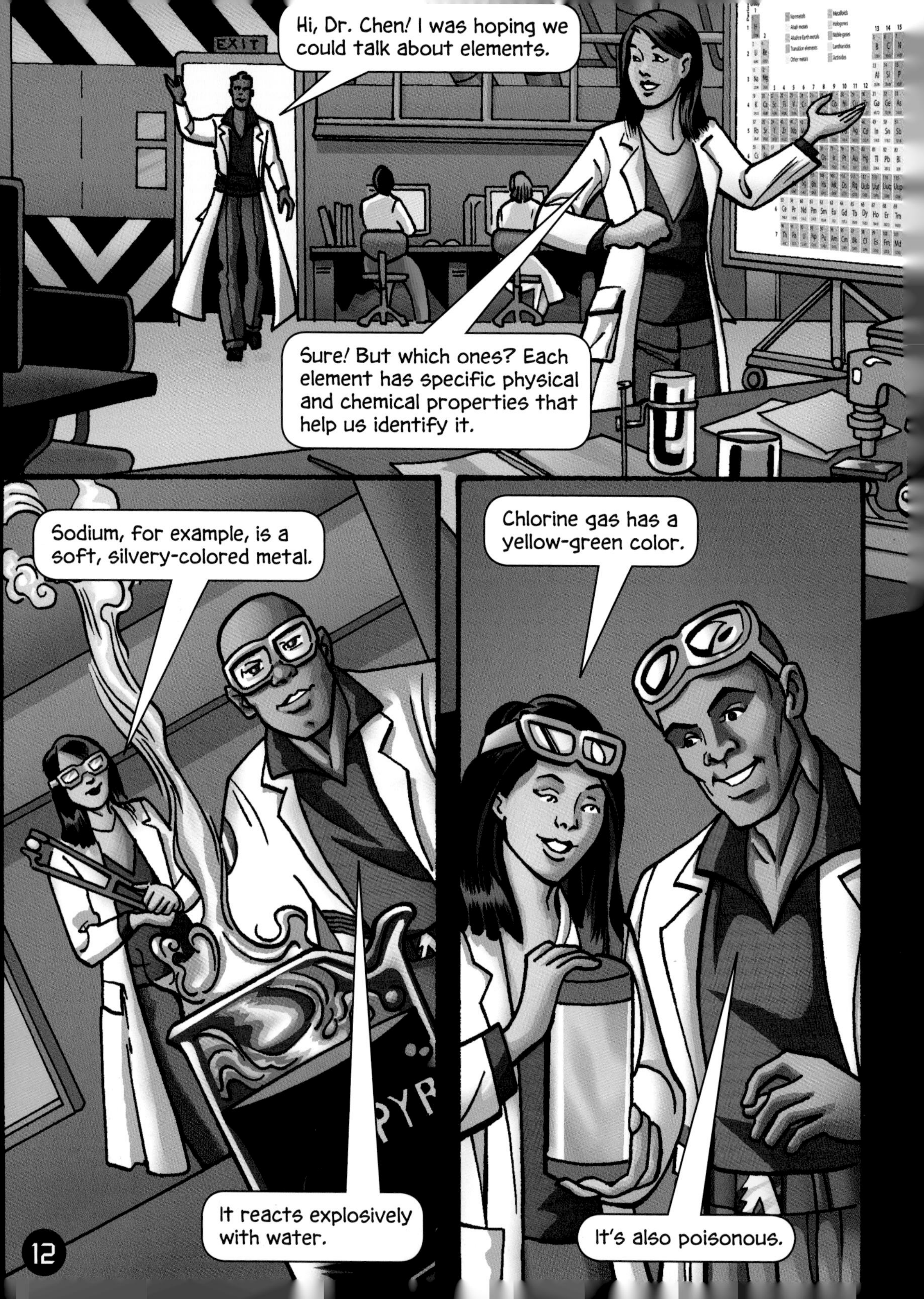
Hi, Dr. Chen! I was hoping we could talk about elements.
Sure! But which ones? Each element has specific physical and chemical properties that help us identify it.
Sodium, for example, is a soft, silvery-colored metal.
It reacts explosively with water.
Chlorine gas has a yellow-green color.
It's also poisonous.

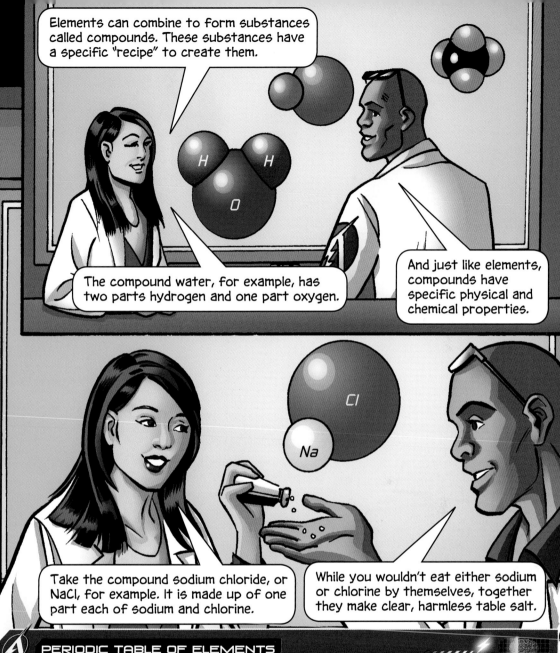

Elements can combine to form substances called compounds. These substances have a specific "recipe" to create them.

H H O

The compound water, for example, has two parts hydrogen and one part oxygen.

And just like elements, compounds have specific physical and chemical properties.

Cl Na

Take the compound sodium chloride, or NaCl, for example. It is made up of one part each of sodium and chlorine.

While you wouldn't eat either sodium or chlorine by themselves, together they make clear, harmless table salt.

PERIODIC TABLE OF ELEMENTS

ACCESS GRANTED: MAX AXIOM

The periodic table of elements lists all the elements. It shows the physical characteristics of each element and helps scientists predict how elements will react when mixed together. On the periodic table, each element has its own symbol. Hydrogen's symbol is H, oxygen's is O, carbon's is C, chlorine's is Cl, and sodium's is Na.

SECTION 3 CHANGING MATTER

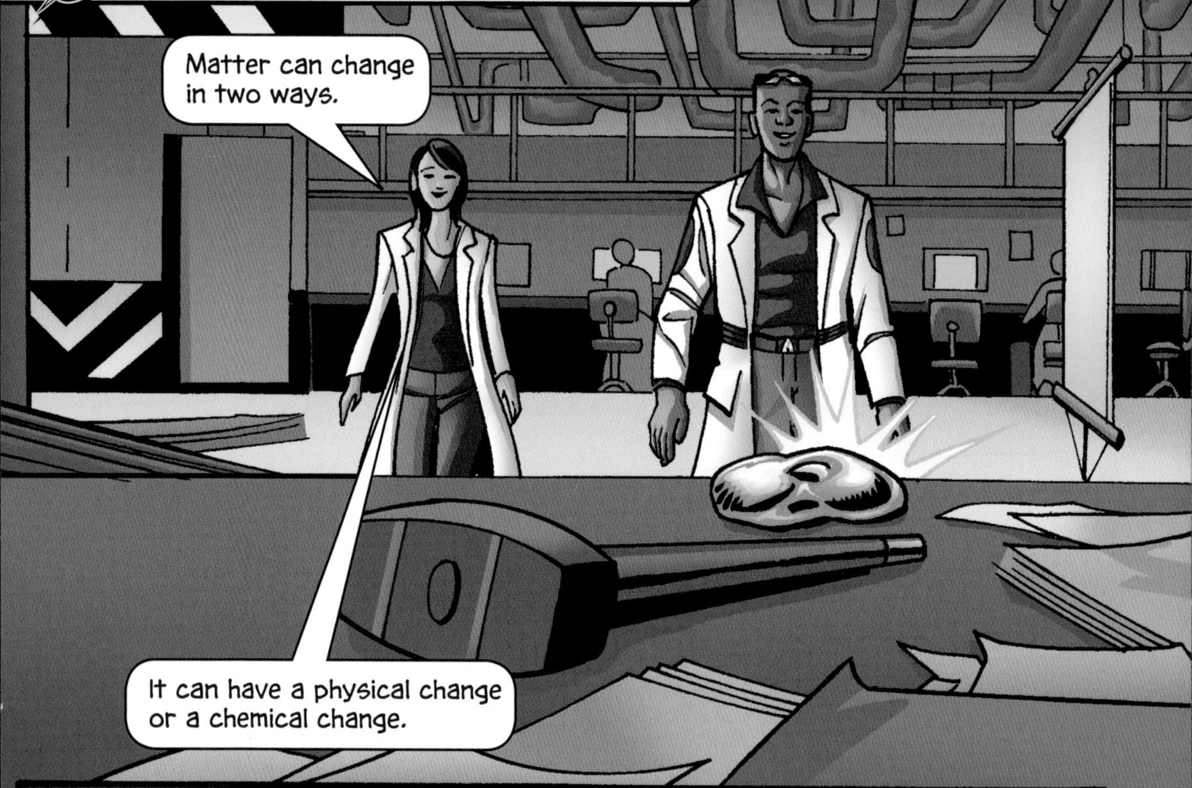

Matter can change in two ways.
It can have a physical change or a chemical change.

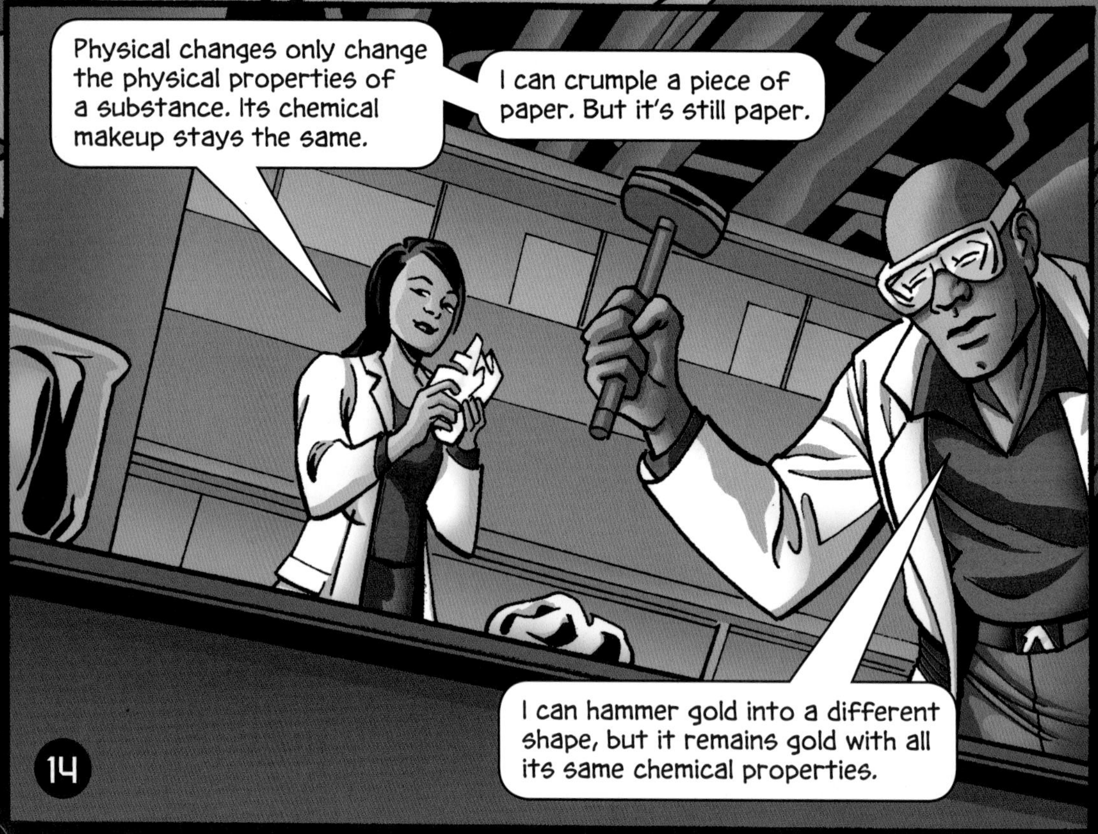

Physical changes only change the physical properties of a substance. Its chemical makeup stays the same.
I can crumple a piece of paper. But it's still paper.
I can hammer gold into a different shape, but it remains gold with all its same chemical properties.

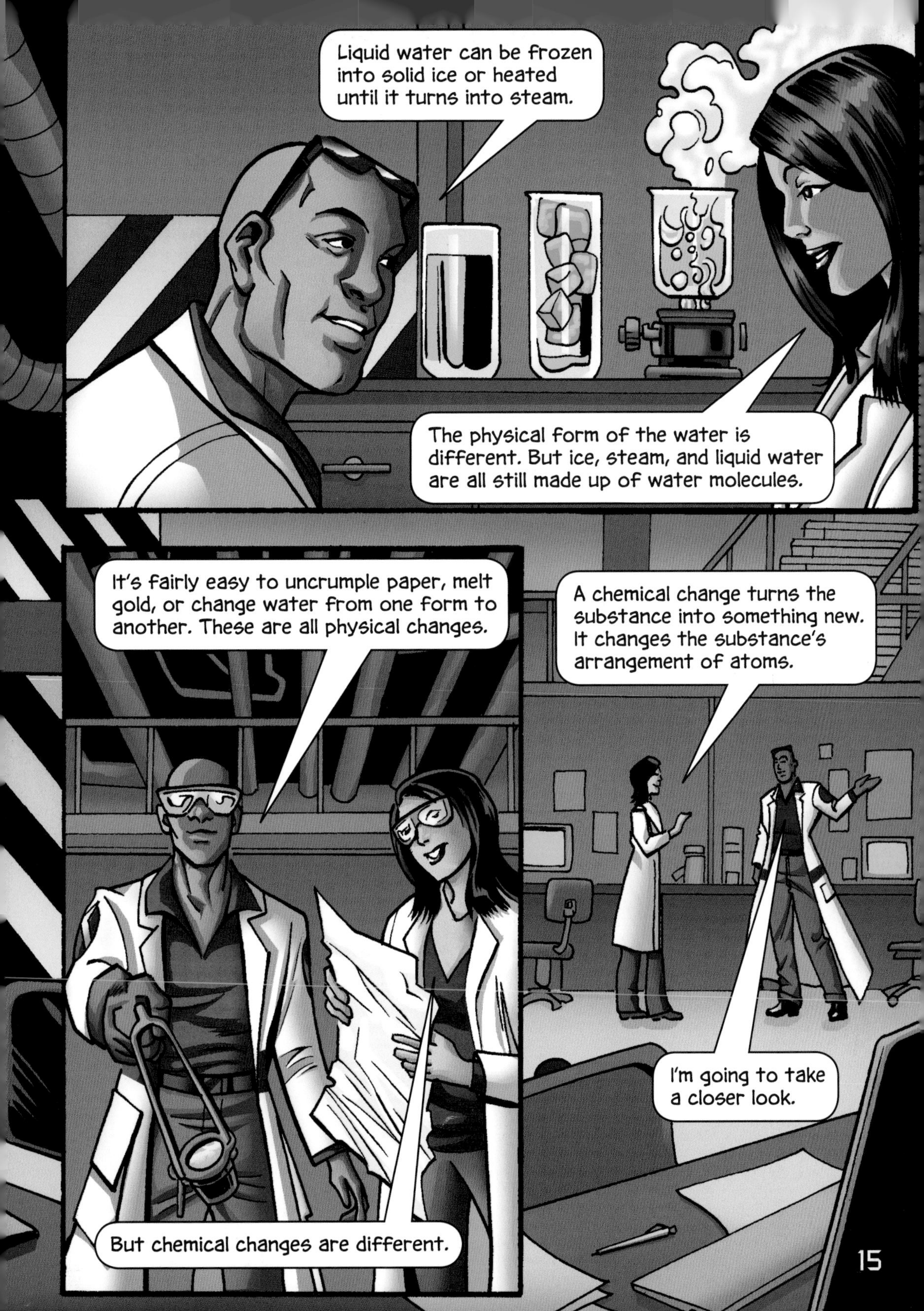
Liquid water can be frozen into solid ice or heated until it turns into steam.
The physical form of the water is different. But ice, steam, and liquid water are all still made up of water molecules.
It's fairly easy to uncrumple paper, melt gold, or change water from one form to another. These are all physical changes.
But chemical changes are different.
A chemical change turns the substance into something new. It changes the substance's arrangement of atoms.
I'm going to take a closer look.

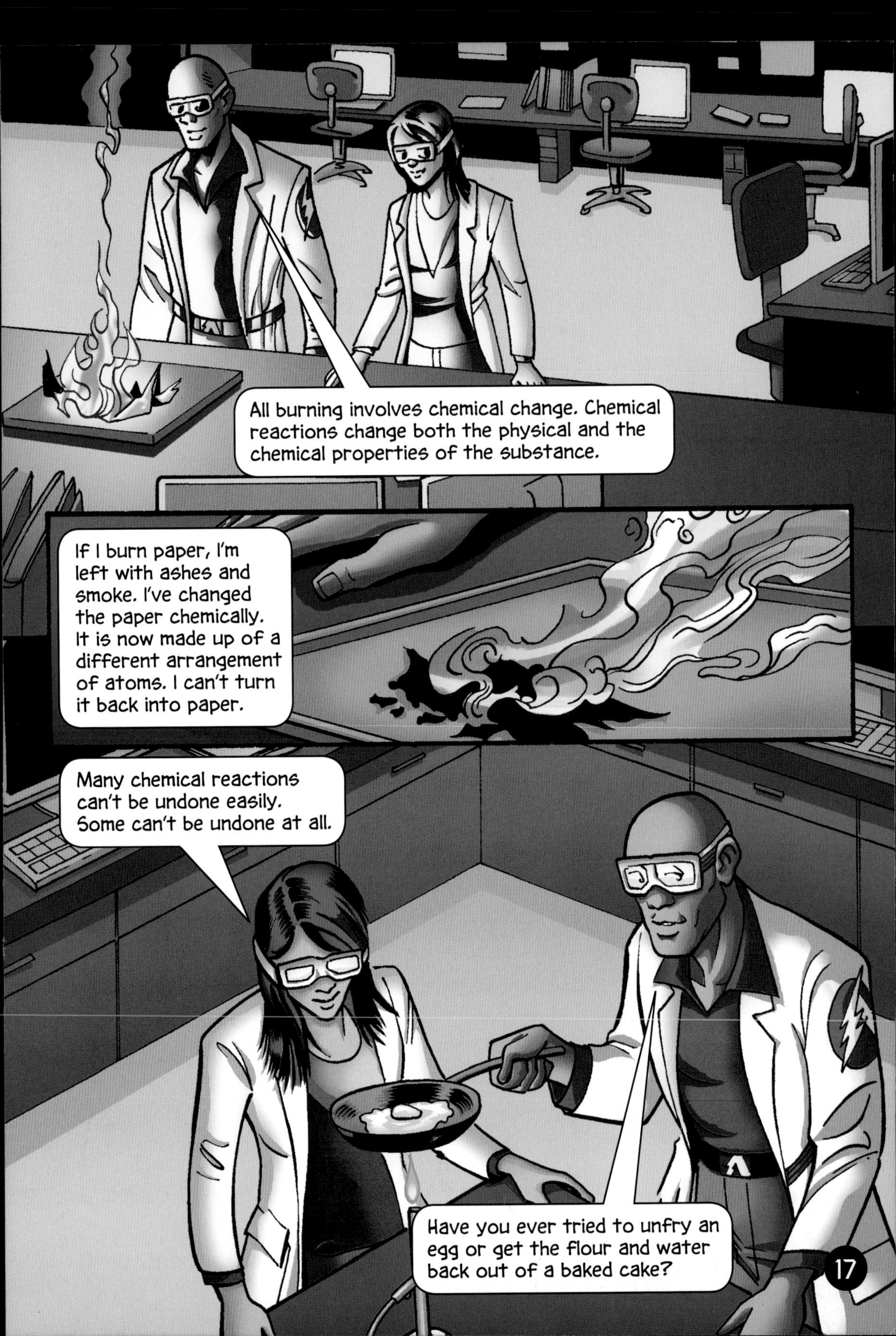
All burning involves chemical change. Chemical reactions change both the physical and the chemical properties of the substance.
If I burn paper, I'm left with ashes and smoke. I've changed the paper chemically. It is now made up of a different arrangement of atoms. I can't turn it back into paper.
Many chemical reactions can't be undone easily. Some can't be undone at all.
Have you ever tried to unfry an egg or get the flour and water back out of a baked cake?

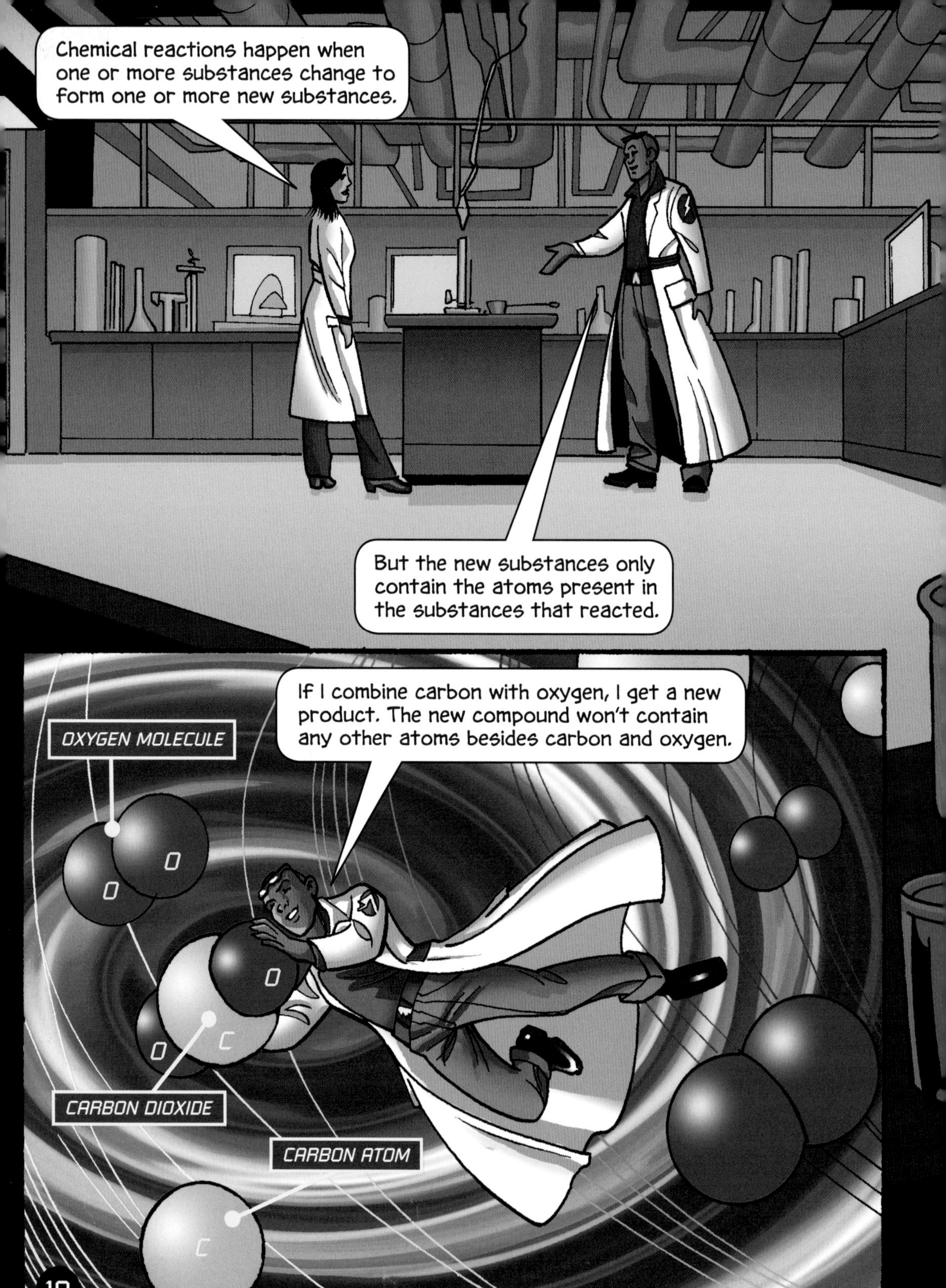
Chemical reactions happen when one or more substances change to form one or more new substances.
But the new substances only contain the atoms present in the substances that reacted.
If I combine carbon with oxygen, I get a new product. The new compound won't contain any other atoms besides carbon and oxygen.
OXYGEN MOLECULE
O
O
O
C
O
CARBON DIOXIDE
CARBON ATOM
C

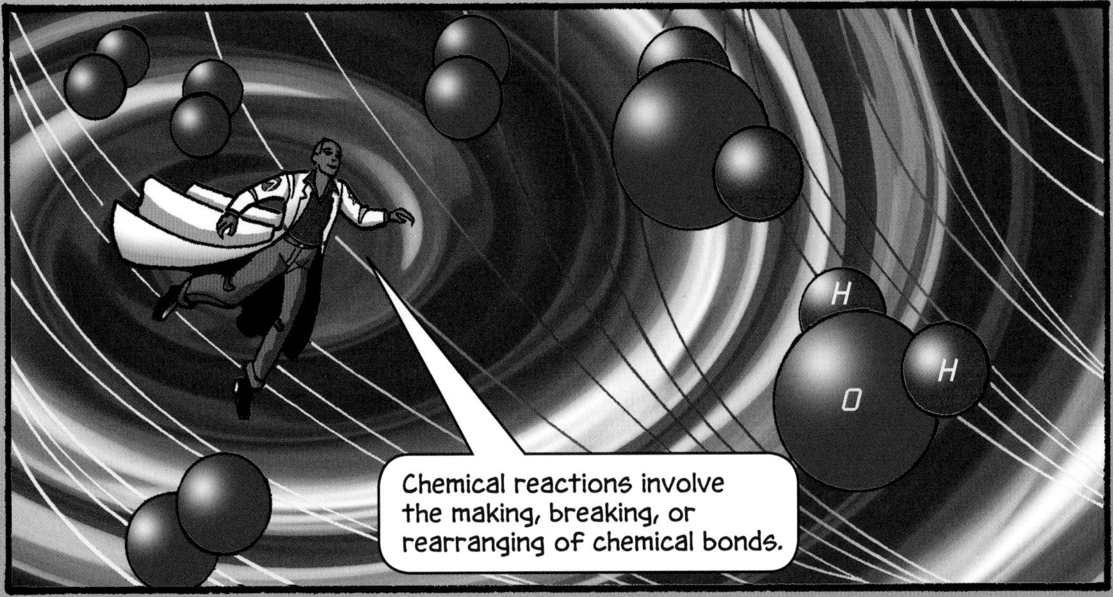
H
H
O
Chemical reactions involve the making, breaking, or rearranging of chemical bonds.

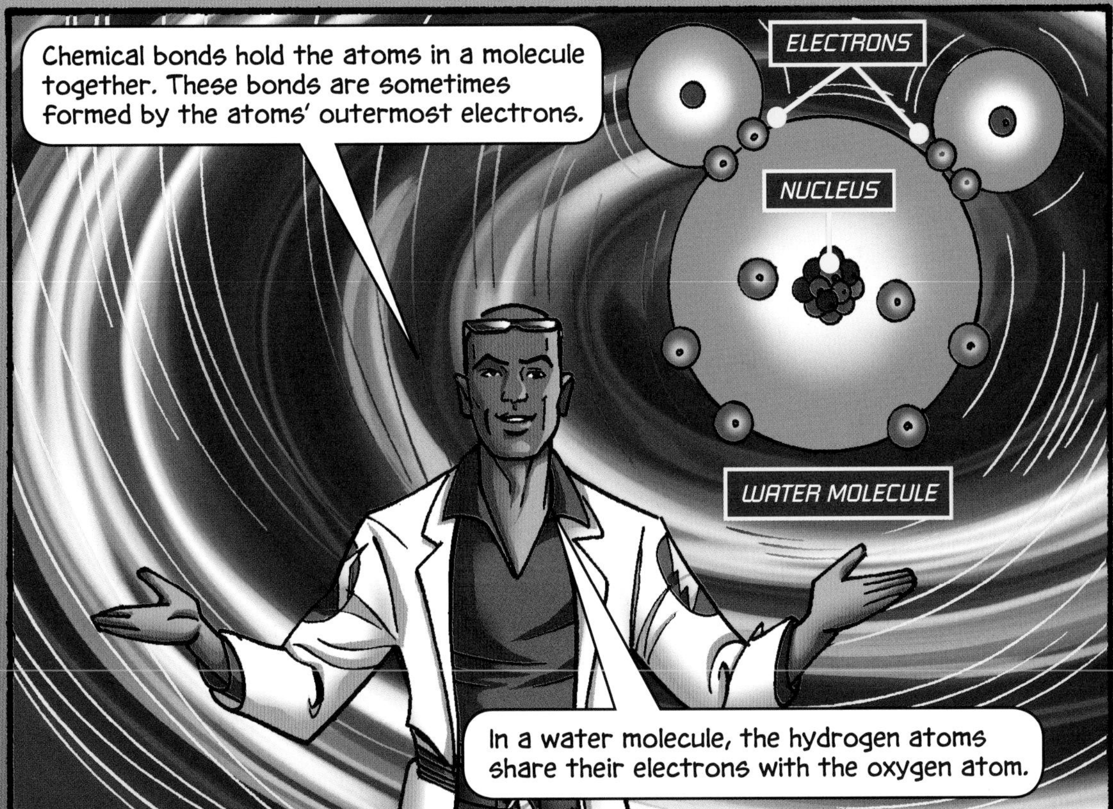
Chemical bonds hold the atoms in a molecule together. These bonds are sometimes formed by the atoms' outermost electrons.
ELECTRONS
NUCLEUS
WATER MOLECULE
In a water molecule, the hydrogen atoms share their electrons with the oxygen atom.

REACTANTS AND PRODUCTS

In a chemical reaction, the substances that undergo a chemical change are called the reactants. The substances that result from the change are called the products.

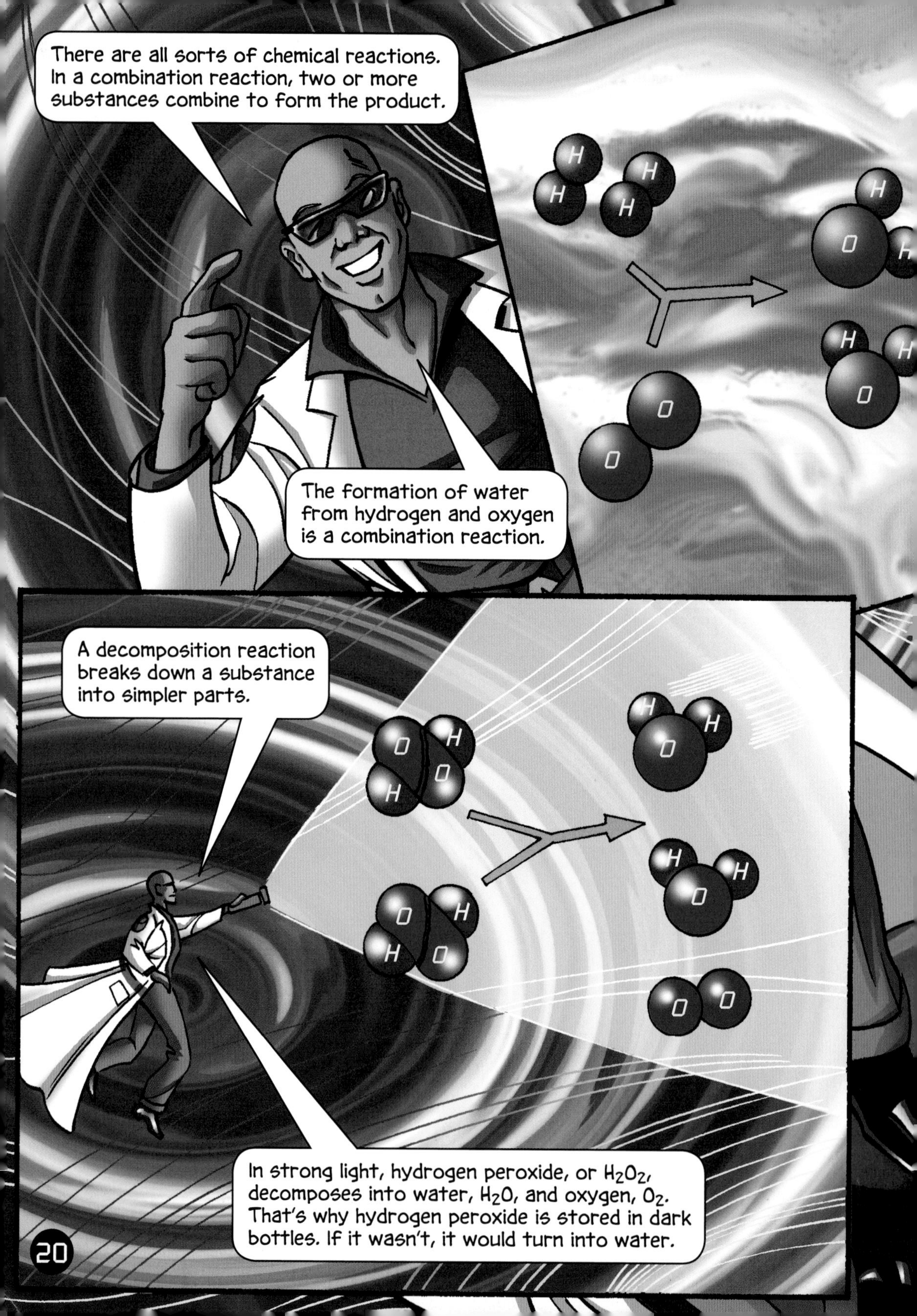
There are all sorts of chemical reactions. In a combination reaction, two or more substances combine to form the product.
The formation of water from hydrogen and oxygen is a combination reaction.
A decomposition reaction breaks down a substance into simpler parts.
In strong light, hydrogen peroxide, or H_2O_2, decomposes into water, H_2O, and oxygen, O_2. That's why hydrogen peroxide is stored in dark bottles. If it wasn't, it would turn into water.

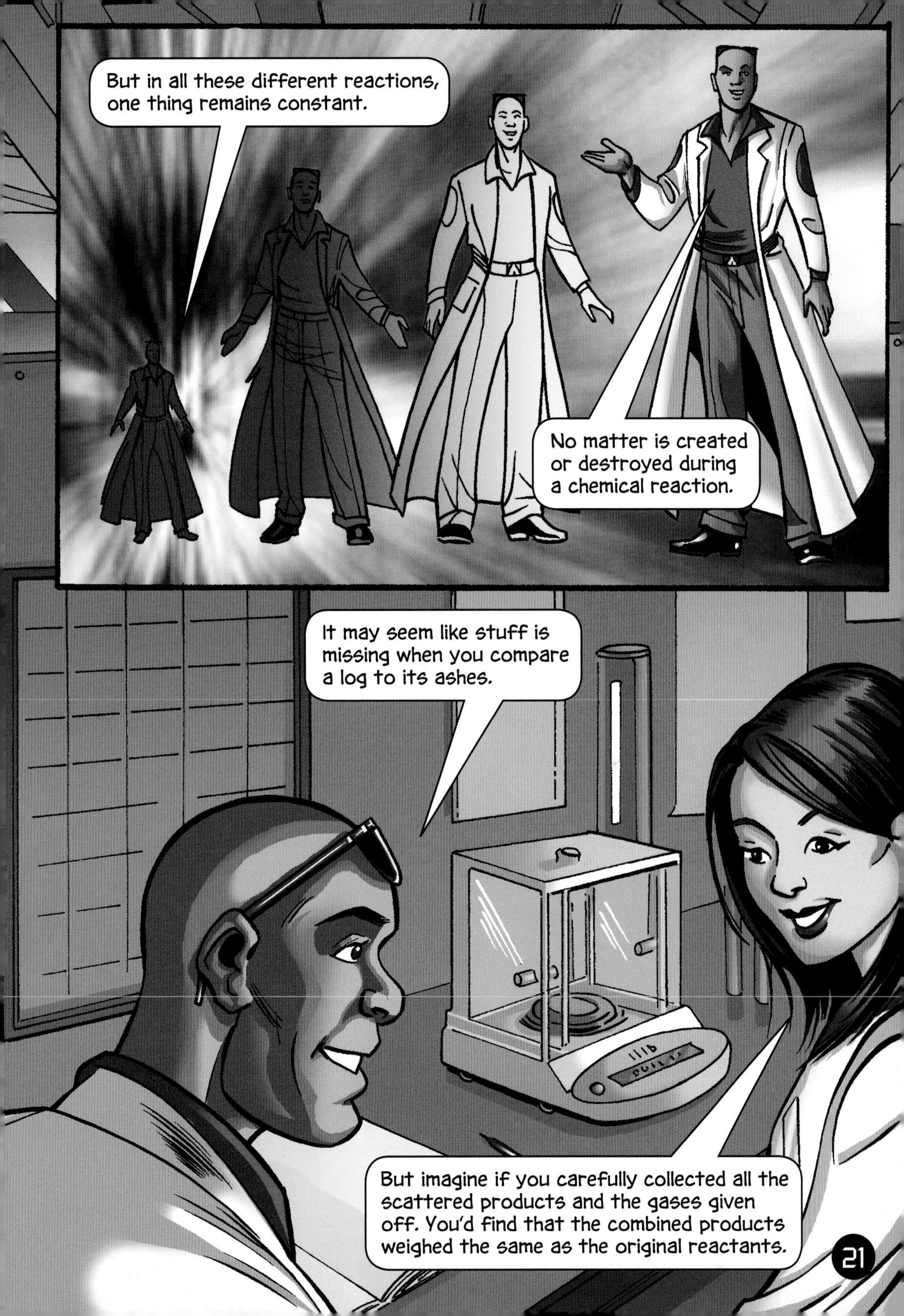
But in all these different reactions, one thing remains constant.
No matter is created or destroyed during a chemical reaction.
It may seem like stuff is missing when you compare a log to its ashes.
But imagine if you carefully collected all the scattered products and the gases given off. You'd find that the combined products weighed the same as the original reactants.

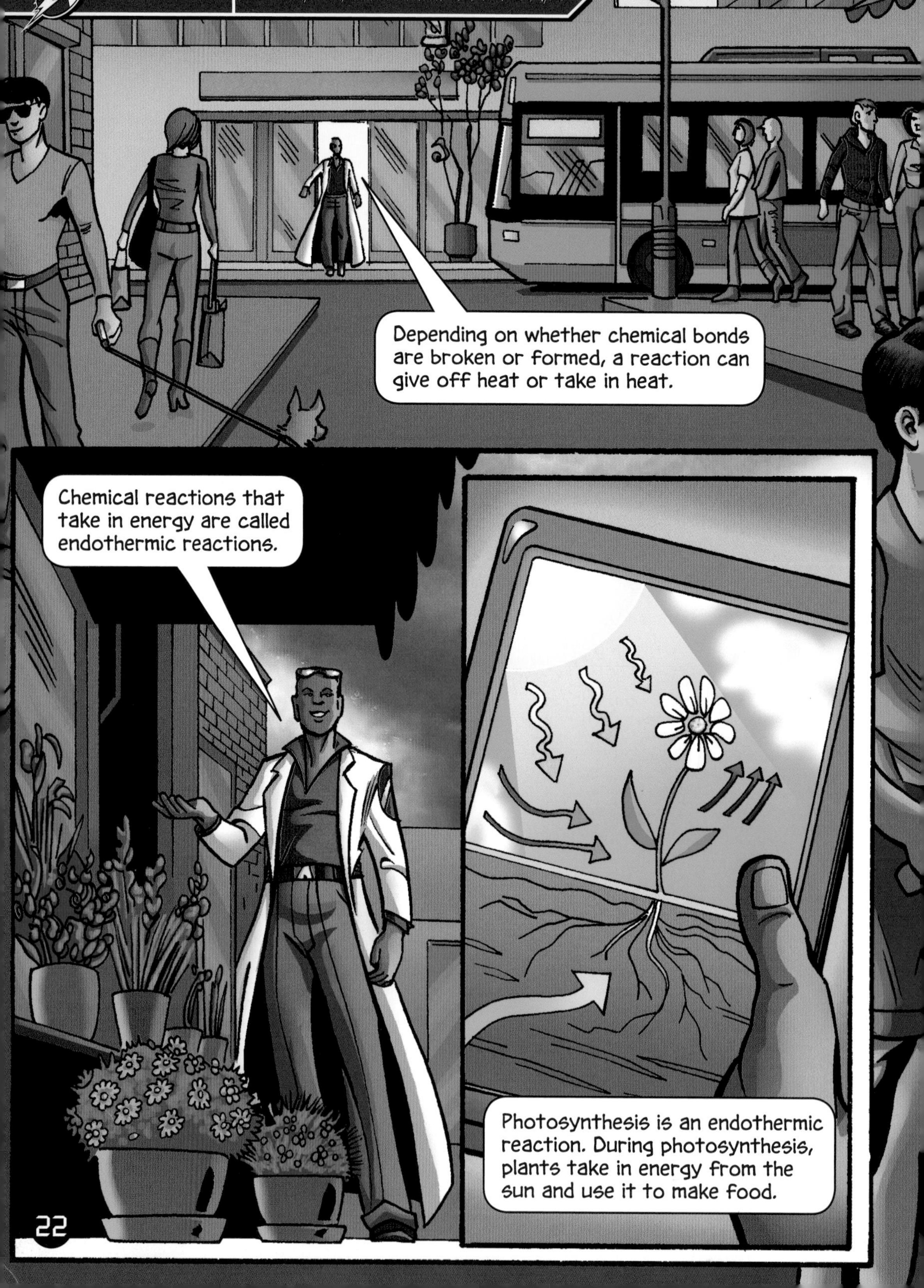
Depending on whether chemical bonds are broken or formed, a reaction can give off heat or take in heat.
Chemical reactions that take in energy are called endothermic reactions.
Photosynthesis is an endothermic reaction. During photosynthesis, plants take in energy from the sun and use it to make food.

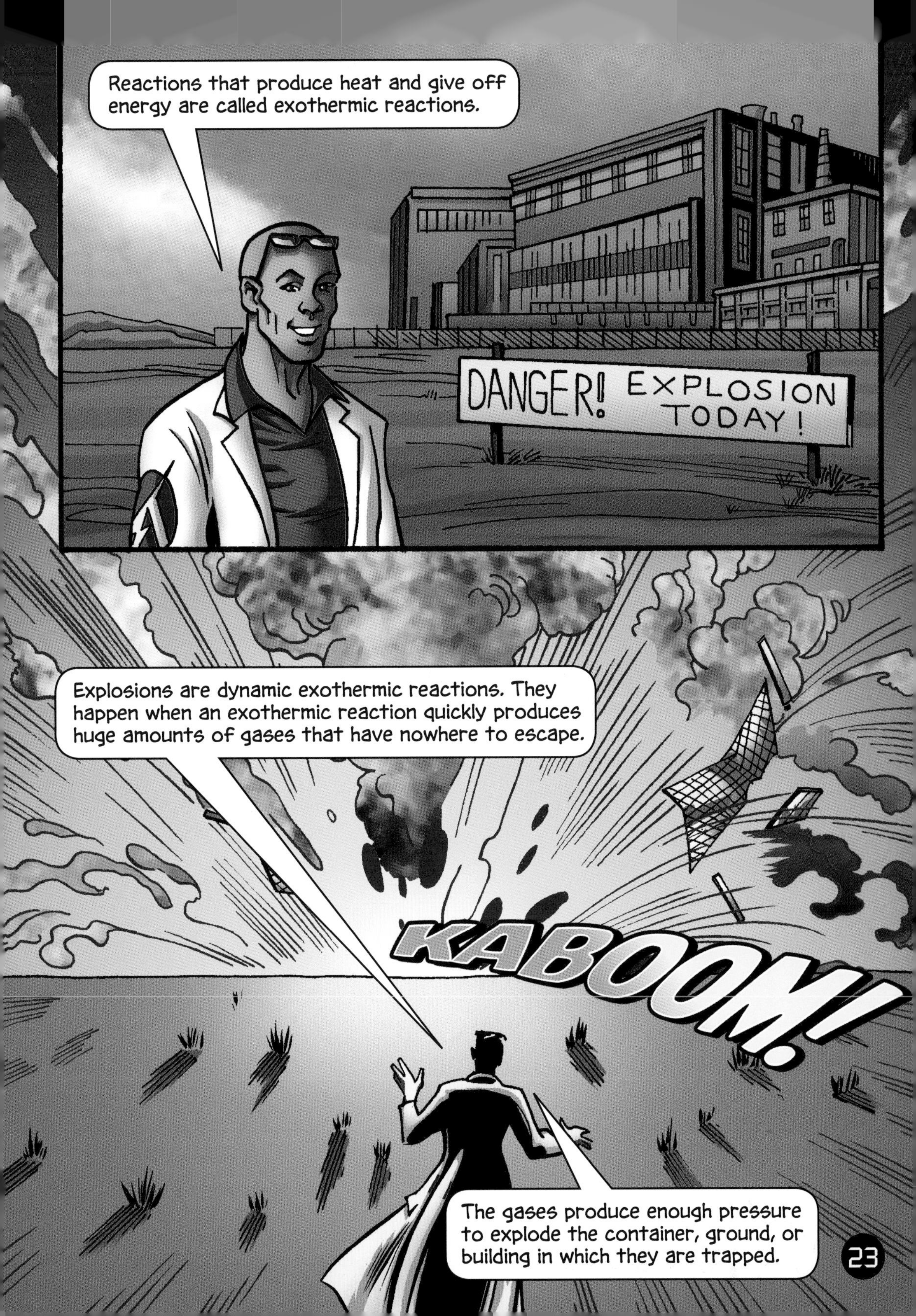
Reactions that produce heat and give off energy are called exothermic reactions.
DANGER! EXPLOSION TODAY!
Explosions are dynamic exothermic reactions. They happen when an exothermic reaction quickly produces huge amounts of gases that have nowhere to escape.
KABOOM!
The gases produce enough pressure to explode the container, ground, or building in which they are trapped.

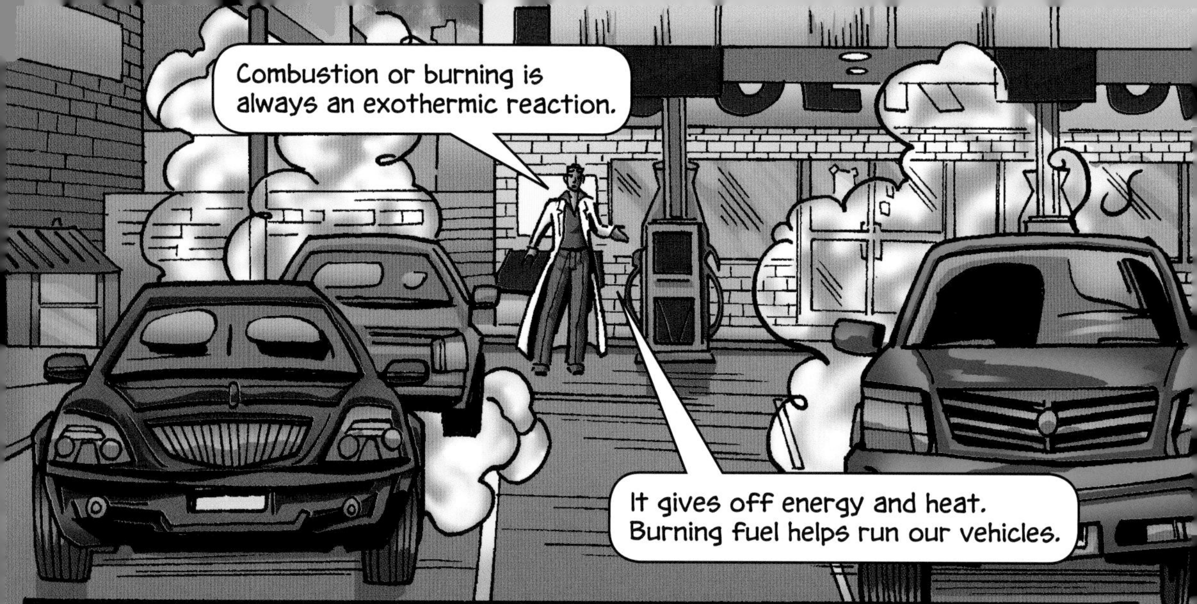
Combustion or burning is always an exothermic reaction.
It gives off energy and heat. Burning fuel helps run our vehicles.

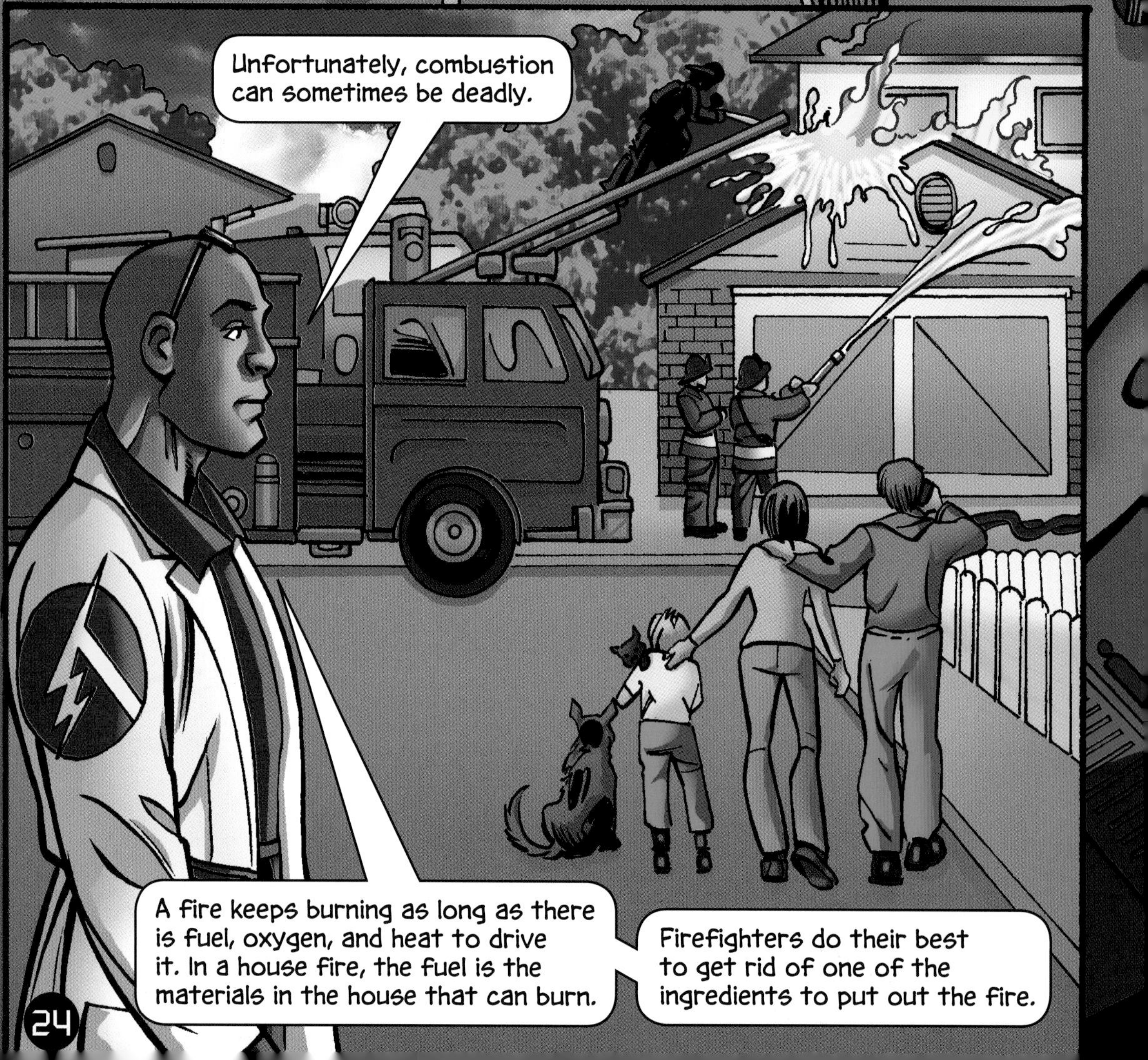
Unfortunately, combustion can sometimes be deadly.
A fire keeps burning as long as there is fuel, oxygen, and heat to drive it. In a house fire, the fuel is the materials in the house that can burn.
Firefighters do their best to get rid of one of the ingredients to put out the fire.

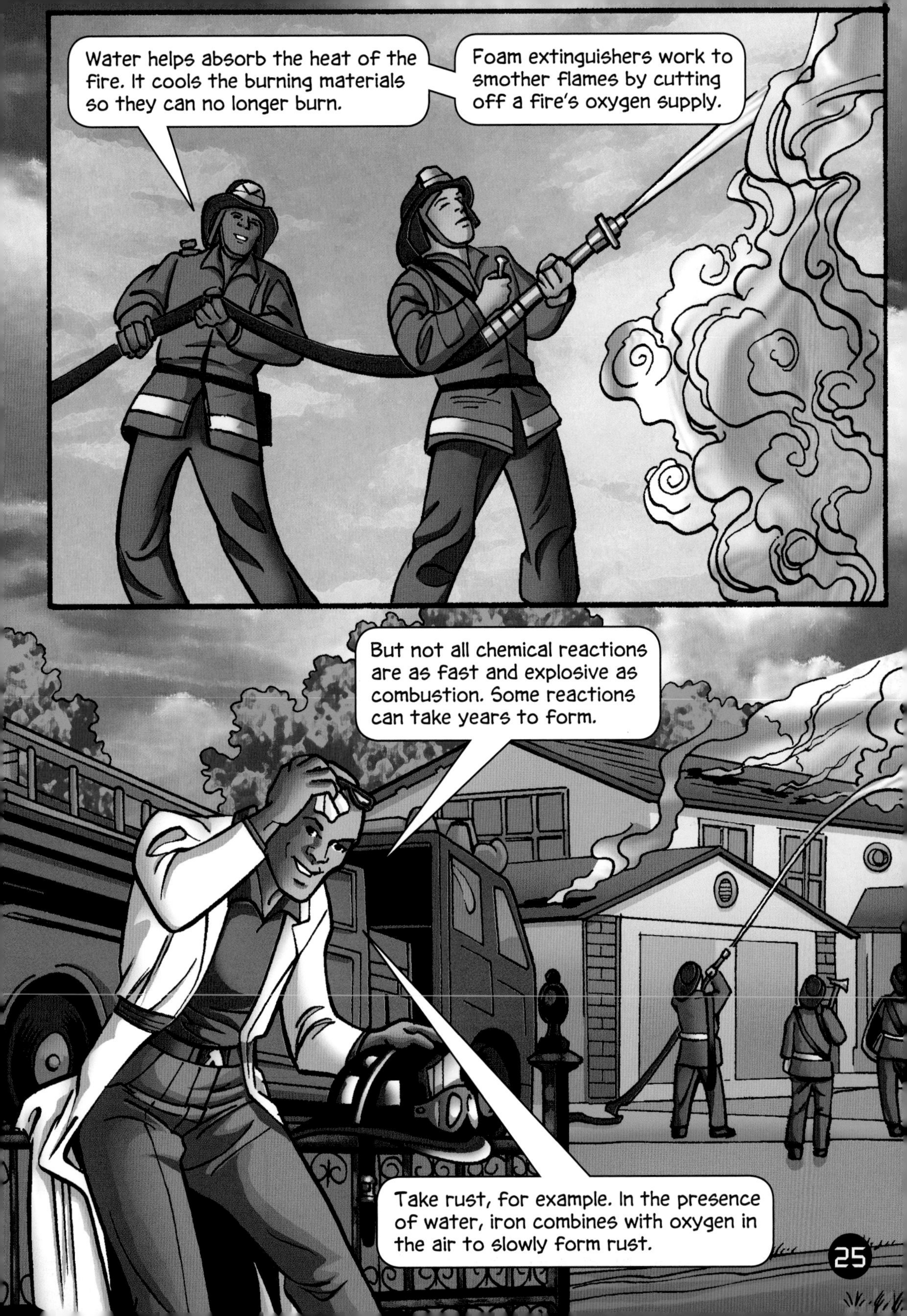
Water helps absorb the heat of the fire. It cools the burning materials so they can no longer burn.
Foam extinguishers work to smother flames by cutting off a fire's oxygen supply.
But not all chemical reactions are as fast and explosive as combustion. Some reactions can take years to form.
Take rust, for example. In the presence of water, iron combines with oxygen in the air to slowly form rust.

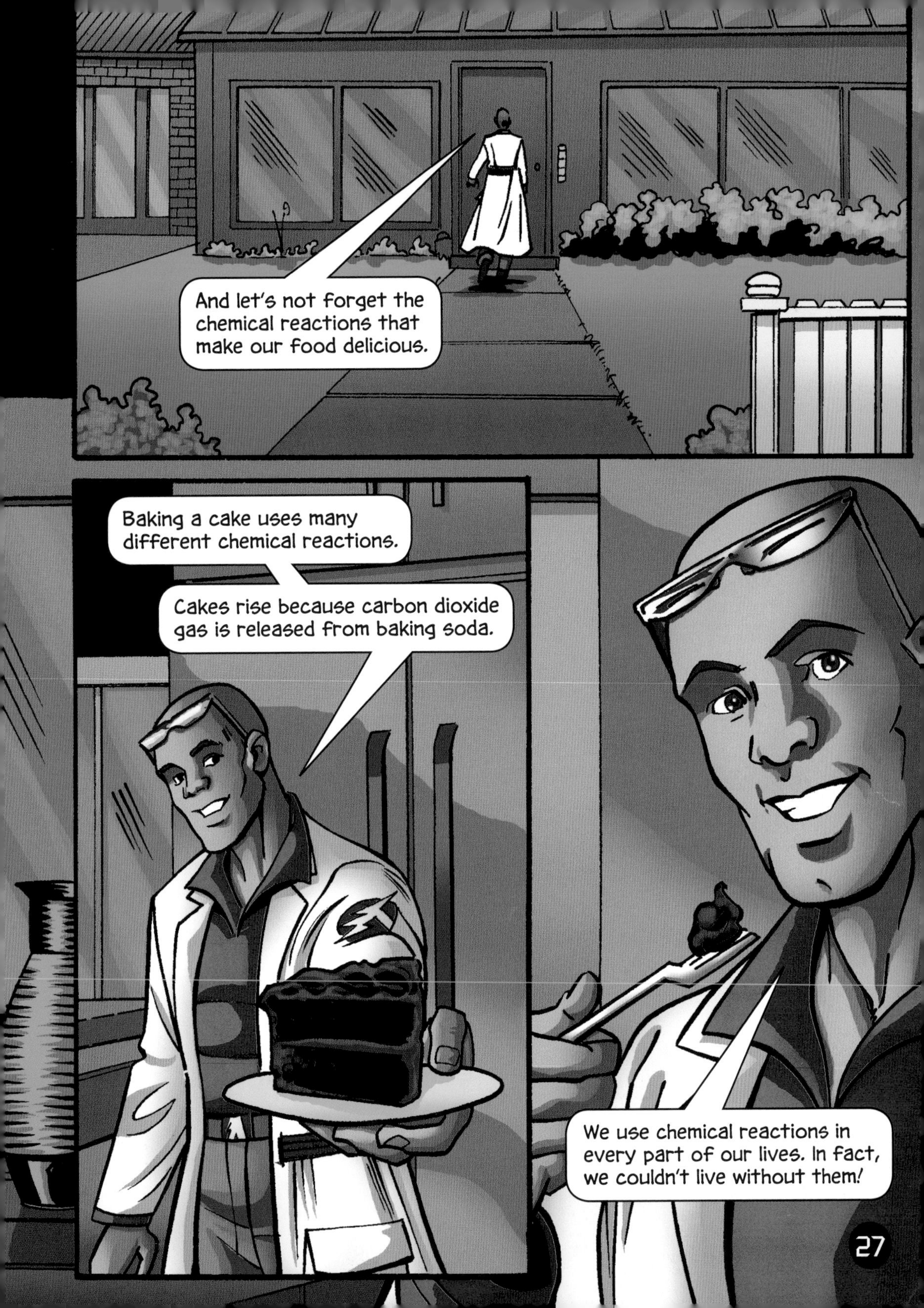
And let's not forget the chemical reactions that make our food delicious.
Baking a cake uses many different chemical reactions.
Cakes rise because carbon dioxide gas is released from baking soda.
We use chemical reactions in every part of our lives. In fact, we couldn't live without them!

CHEMICAL REACTIONS

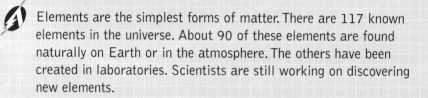

Elements are the simplest forms of matter. There are 117 known elements in the universe. About 90 of these elements are found naturally on Earth or in the atmosphere. The others have been created in laboratories. Scientists are still working on discovering new elements.

A molecular formula tells you the total number and kinds of atoms in a molecule. Water's molecular formula is H_2O. That means to make a molecule of water you need two atoms of hydrogen (H) and one atom of oxygen (O). Carbon dioxide's formula is CO_2. That means you'd need one atom of carbon (C) and two of oxygen (O) to make a carbon dioxide molecule.

Fireflies glow because of a special reaction involving oxygen atoms and two other chemicals. The chemical reaction takes place in the firefly's abdomen. The light produced shines right through its body.

Heating chemical compounds produces the beautiful colors you see in fireworks. When heated, the compounds give off colors. To get blue, fireworks experts add copper compounds. To get orange, they add calcium.

New York's Statue of Liberty is green thanks to chemical reactions. Made of copper, the statue was originally the color of a penny. But over the years, the copper has reacted with oxygen in the air, or oxidized, to form the statue's famous green coating.

Have you ever made a volcano using baking soda and vinegar? The resulting "lava" is made by a chemical reaction. The baking soda and vinegar react to produce water, sodium acetate, and lots of fizzy carbon dioxide gas.

 Acid rain is caused by sulfur dioxide and nitrogen oxides that are released into the atmosphere by human pollution or natural events. These chemicals react with water, oxygen, and other compounds to form acid rain. Acid rain has harmful effects on the environment, wildlife, and humans.

MORE ABOUT

SUPER SCIENTIST

Real name: Maxwell J. Axiom
Hometown: Seattle, Washington
Height: 6' 1"   **Weight:** 192 lbs
Eyes: Brown   **Hair:** None

Super capabilities: Super intelligence; able to shrink to the size of an atom; sunglasses give x-ray vision; lab coat allows for travel through time and space.

Origin: Since birth, Max Axiom seemed destined for greatness. His mother, a marine biologist, taught her son about the mysteries of the sea. His father, a nuclear physicist and volunteer park ranger, schooled Max on the wonders of earth and sky.

One day on a wilderness hike, a megacharged lightning bolt struck Max with blinding fury. When he awoke, Max discovered a newfound energy and set out to learn as much about science as possible. He traveled the globe earning degrees in every aspect of the field. Upon his return, he was ready to share his knowledge and new identity with the world. He had become Max Axiom, Super Scientist.

GLOSSARY

atom (AT-uhm)—an element in its smallest form

combination reaction (kom-buh-NAY-shuhn ree-AK-shuhn)—a chemical reaction where two substances combine to form a new product

combustion (kuhm-BUS-chuhn)—the process of catching fire and burning

compound (KOM-pound)—something formed by combining two or more parts

decomposition reaction (dee-kom-poh-ZIH-shuhn ree-AK-shuhn)—a chemical reaction where a substance breaks down into simpler parts

electron (i-LEK-tron)—a tiny particle in an atom that travels around the nucleus

element (E-luh-muhnt)—a basic substance in chemistry that cannot be broken down into simpler substances under ordinary lab conditions

endothermic reaction (en-doh-THUR-mic ree-AK-shuhn)—a chemical reaction that takes in energy

exothermic reaction (eks-oh-THUR-mic ree-AK-shuhn)—a chemical reaction that gives off energy

fermentation (fur-men-TAY-shuhn)—a chemical change that makes the sugar in a substance change into alcohol

matter (MAT-ur)—anything that has weight and takes up space

molecule (MOL-uh-kyool)—two or more atoms of the same or different elements that have bonded; a molecule is the smallest part of a substance that can't be divided without a chemical change

READ MORE

Brent, Lynnette. *Chemical Changes.* Why Chemistry Matters. New York: Crabtree Publishing Company, 2009.

Hoffman, Mary Ann. *Scientific Inquiry in Action: Chemical Reaction!* Science Scope. New York: PowerKids Press, 2009.

Lew, Kristi. *Chemical Reactions.* Essential Chemistry. New York: Chelsea House Publishers, 2008.

Oxlade, Chris. *Material Changes and Reactions.* Chemicals in Action. Chicago: Heinemann Library, 2007.

Solway, Andrew. *From Gunpowder to Laser Chemistry: Discovering Chemical Reactions.* Chain Reactions. Chicago: Heinemann Library, 2007.

INTERNET SITES

FactHound offers a safe, fun way to find Internet sites related to this book. All of the sites on FactHound have been researched by our staff.

Here's all you do:

Visit *www.facthound.com*

Type in this code: 9781429647724

acid rain, 29
atoms, 9, 10–11, 13, 15, 16,
    17, 18, 19, 28

burning, 4, 7, 17, 24, 25

carbon, 11, 13, 18, 28
carbon dioxide, 6, 11, 18, 27,
    28, 29
chemical bonds, 19, 22
chlorine, 12, 13
combination reactions, 20
combustion. *See* burning
compounds, 13, 18, 28, 29
copper, 11, 28

decomposition reactions, 20
digestion, 6, 26

electrons, 9, 19
elements, 11, 12–13, 28
endothermic reactions, 22
energy, 22, 23, 24
exothermic reactions, 23, 24
explosions, 23

fermentation, 6
fire, 4–5, 6, 24–25
fireflies, 5, 28
fireworks, 5, 7, 28

gunpowder, 7

heat, 15, 22, 23, 24, 25, 28
hydrogen, 10, 13, 16, 19,
    20, 28
hydrogen peroxide, 16, 20

matter, 8–9, 11, 14, 21, 28
molecules, 9, 10, 11, 15, 16,
    19, 28

oxygen, 10, 11, 13, 16, 18,
    19, 20, 24, 25, 28, 29

periodic table of elements, 13
photosynthesis, 22
physical changes, 14–15
products, 18, 19, 20, 21

reactants, 19, 21
rust, 25

sodium, 12, 13
sodium chloride, 13
Statue of Liberty, 28

table salt. *See* sodium
    chloride

water, 10, 13, 15, 16, 17, 19,
    20, 25, 28, 29